THE MARCHES

THE MARCHES
James Scully

A BOOK OF POEMS

HOLT, RINEHART AND WINSTON

NEW YORK   CHICAGO   SAN FRANCISCO

I'm deeply grateful to the Ingram Merrill Foundation for enabling me to spend a year abroad. Many friends have made useful suggestions, but none to greater effect than John Malcolm Brinnin, my teacher; and, more recently, George Amabile.

Published simultaneously in Canada by Holt, Rinehart and Winston of Canada, Ltd.

Library of Congress Catalog Card Number: 67-19045

The following poems appeared originally in THE NEW YORKER: *The Glass Blower, A Late Spring, Midsummer, Gibraltar, A Fantasy of Little Waters, Crew Practice on Lake Bled, in Jugoslavia,* and *The Grandson.*

A Fantasy of Little Waters appears in this volume under the title, *Enter: The Waters,* and *Crew Practice on Lake Bled, in Jugoslavia* appears here as *Crew Practice.*

The following poems appeared originally in POETRY: *The Change of Life* and *Conception is a blessing.*

Conception is a blessing appears here as *Aubade.*

Other poems in this volume appeared originally in THE CRITICAL QUARTERLY, HIKA, FINE ARTS MAGAZINE, THE WORMWOOD REVIEW, and THE PENNY PAPER.

The fragment from Archilochus is reprinted here in a translation by Richmond Lattimore (GREEK LYRICS, University of Chicago Press), by permission of the University of Chicago Press.

Designed by Paul Bacon
8655300
Printed in the United States of America
Second Edition

For Arlene

Contents

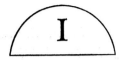

I

The Angel in the Church of
St. John the Baptist

I, I could unfold you a story.

But now, through dawn, the tiered marble drips
evergreen branches, now I worry
into Christmas. Underfoot, the crypt's
bundled into quilts of green, of red
poinsettia. And toward these eyes, dressed
in gold brocade day descends (this head,
these wings & feet, stone, weary of rest
among perennials

The Glass Blower

Canaries were his hobby.
Upstairs in the attic, with his knobby
hands, he put up small-gauge wire stalls;
copper gauze, from the slant roof to the floor,
huddled the birdflock in their drowsy ark.
There were a hundred or more
that sat on crusted bars, their claws locked tight,
upright albino bats, until the night-
time came. When he groped up the stairs, the light
blazed and they awoke.
The hungry bodies quickened.
A few flew at the screen, but every dark
reflection glided skillfully on the walls
behind the gold wheelings: wheels of a clock
chirping every second on the second.

Gradually it unwound.
Then going to work, a Jonah's underground,
he'd disappear into a warehouse: punch in,
check orders, stir a batch of sand, start
the wheel grinding out his daily payload
of undistracted art—
and shape a universe, a toy glass ball
one shakes, seeing the plastic snowflakes fall
within a pool, upon a parasol
of plastic (underneath
a woman and a man
were frozen in their strolling). And the haloed
high-stooled glass blower, leaning over a Bunsen
burner, at a wooden bench, would breathe
glass straws into strings of glass balloons.

They were sold—the rare
canaries, then pigeons, chickens, and a pair
of guinea pigs. Experiments, they arrived
and left, like courses in their covered dish.
He even bred, in an aquarium,
rainbow-colored fish:
then, streaked with orange scars, the slim swordtails
cut a wakeless way, and the milky sails
of angelfish, razor-thin, edged trails
of tendril over rock;
the snails neither sank
nor swam, but stuffed their pinkish horns with scum.
He also stocked black mollies. Short-lived,
their bulbous heads and tapering bodies, black
tear-shapes, cruised the bottom of the tank.

　　Lightheaded bubbles swirled
surfacewise. Wound in a filmy world,
a fetus feeding on its inmost part,
he'd circle bar to bar each night, without
going far, but staggering home stone blind,
his pockets inside-out.
Fleeced, he made the cellar workshop a cage
of pipes and copper coils, trying to gauge
the distillation and advancing age
of alcohol. Ferment-
ing, dribbling from the lips,
he would sit walleyed with his reeling mind
among odd junk. Near a dog-eared sea chart
a bottle, like a toppled monument,
preserved the leavings of a model ship.

The Change of Life

Into what silence had your still life cried?
You seemed unchanged, yet were becoming new,
a mirror mild with steam. A winter's bride
like snow that stays, a moment, on the sea.

. . . Sorrow, the water taps gushed from their worn
mouths; the loose slip wrinkled like a snake-
skin pouring from your thighs. And being born
childless, your moistening body woke.

Recovering in the bath, you were amazed
to find the lifelong wound without a scar;
and fearless as a child, with nothing on,
you watched the cooling fog.

                      And the cleared air
disclosed those papered walls, and cold sweat glazed
the black-and-white engraving of a swan.

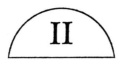

II

"Aimai-je un rêve?"

Then what is possible?
We parted in the garden.
Stunned, I walk through town
with a heart the gas fumes harden.
Thunder trucks throb on
but rain does not come down,
and I'm insoluble . . .
Flower, false or true,
loved I a dream, or you?

Whatever was the case—
I, the man who dreamt
he was a butterfly,
or butterfly who dreamt
he was a man—I sigh,
hoping each lovely lie
survives, a kind of grace,
and that walking wide awake
is not the real mistake.

A Late Spring

Childheart, time alone is not enough.
Life waits. Over-sized snowflakes start to fall
past the spring deadline . . .

      This morning, driving home for Easter,
I saw two mares the color of burnt chestnut
browsing in a sloping meadow.
Ankle deep in the fresh snow
they walked awkwardly about in it, and hesitated—
sore-thumb, Negro horses in a world of light,
a mirage of low lying cotton blossom
cushioning their hooves.

You could almost hear
lost gods breathing in the earth . . .
One following the other, sway-backed,
they nudged the soft snow,
their flexible lips and barely opened teeth
seizing the sweet grass, the withered needle-stalks,
the roots shaken with water and dirt
torn from a long sleep.

Aubade

But know how daylight wavers on the sill
flooding the ruined air—how slithering
the great nightcrawlers gather in themselves,
and hungry sparrows are gasping at their fill
and the worms still turning, pieces quivering
of arrested motion—how breaking into halves
from woolen blankets we wake shivering,
a man and woman still
whose bodies want the warmth, two rank shorn sheep
whose fluffy folds have drifted to the wolves—
and how our minds are turning back to sleep,
our thoughts to peace: the one gigantic will
unsexed, and deathly still.

Enter: The Waters

And cirrus rush of surf is blown
away, off-colors of the sky;
still rootless, vaguely yellowish,
a protoplasmic jellyfish
sporting one dark spot, floats by,
suspended like a burnt-out sun.

"One evening, when our daughter turns
the faucet on, we'll kiss her hands
until they shiver with deep concerns
unearthed, straying where she stands;
and she will shake the feeling off,
shaking her hair at all the bother
of fixing it; and hear a cough
drifting from a distant room
like thickening waters, and will assume
it wasn't she, it was another.

With fingers grown from coral shelves,
one morning, those clear hands will groom
loose strands, the veins of platinum
distend, their blowzy breaths become
the clouds, flooding her nails—the comb
fathoming her flowing selves."

Gibraltar

I've never seen it. I have only heard
sheer legend of a fat leviathan,
the British butting-head off fascist Spain
and guardian to the Mediterranean,
blue garden of the earth—of how a brain-
gray myth lifts like a mountain from the seas,
unscaled, a mooring for the barnacle,
for few stone pine and wild olive trees
grasping its limestone back, insoluble
so far. A Pillar of Hercules! I've seen
newswire photos of the rock's endurance,
flat dots amassing dead ideas, which mean
the promising Prudential Life Insurance
Company of America, the word.

But if I've never seen the thing itself
I may imagine it: a pockmarked bomb
shelter the seagulls grip like ugly doves,
or human hive, each probing honeycomb
swollen with machinery, and droves
of lives. Its sphinx eyes hide artillery;
destroyers glide like ducks before the blind,
their topsides deadpan, all activity
below the waterline. And at the hind-
side of Gibraltar turns a gentle slope,
I'm told, of whitewashed homes with garden flowers
growing; and steel stems and fingers grope
cliffside, set to expose a rose of hours,
the stone afire, gathering itself.

III

Midsummer

(Coventry, Connecticut)

That the high sheen of death could blot
this green away, or life survive
the great ice age, is almost not

to be believed. Clearly, today's
raw sunlight ripens into grass
and grazing cows, as though always

it has been so. Still, glacial rock
like giant bone pokes through the earth
and weighs the age-old walls that block

these fields, the livestock locked within.
A herd of motley, whites and blacks,
the cows browse in oblivion,

their muscles ruffling under veils
of gaudy, violet-winged black flies
aswarm their hides—and swish their tails,

thickset, but limber as bullwhips
perpetually in motion, long
quick lengths unraveled at the tips,

from side to side. Nearby, a brace
of mules tethered to iron stakes
stand stock-still. And out through space,

at times, too far away to hear,
a flashing Sabre-jet transcends
the mules, the massive cows—a mere

slow-motioned slip of silver light—
and wakes a ghostly rainbow arc
flatly across far hills, its slight

exhaustion burning through the blue
useless sky, trailing away,
its destination out of view.

The glacier's gone. The cows assent
grassward, earmarked with metal tags,
delicacies of ornament

that glint and tick away the sun
as their ears twitch, as they remain
one pulsing mass—as if each one

had undergone the bull, the calf,
the frost-bit rains, and now held out
for nothing less than life itself:

such middle-aging gaiety
as knows not what it was, nor is,
nor what it is about to be,

nor cares that space thins out, goes dumb,
that time may cease to come—as if,
rockbound, this were the kingdom come,

and the hunched fields were crystal-clear
Jerusalem, and life was judged
vibration in the summer air.

An American Airman
(Northern France)

Armed Forces Day. Beyond Verdun
whole families of Frogs popped up
to catch the show, the western sun.

Police dogs worrying the leash
kicked off the trials, and masters jogged
past hurdles with their dogs, with each

one strained. Mounting a mock attack
four aged F-84's cold-cocked
the runway. The line doubled back

a final time. One peeled rank,
climbed, and lobbing a napalm can
knocked out a non-existent tank.

Loudspeakers droned. A common prop
plane wound around the cloudline, where
a sky diver started to drop

end over end, until the plum-
meting man jerked in a half stop,
then tipped, rocked like a pendulum

over us all. Orange and white
his blown-up parachute, mushroomed,
comes bumbling down. But it's too late

to see him through. Queued autos slip
by the guard gate. Only the main
control tower above the airstrip

remains: held over the flagstaff,
hard up, like a landlocked lighthouse
green-lighting nothing but itself,

for which it stands. Logged shadows wade
deeper in darkness, the airshow
out like a light. We have played

games that become our life, and why
the C.O. knows. I've dreamt of life
driving all night toward Paris, high

as a kite, higher still, and not
a soul in sight—just stars and air
and passing time. Nobody thought

stars gave a damn. But when all's through
that's not the point, though it's the truth.
We simply wished: to brawl, to screw

the Frogs, lose ourselves in the flood-
lit Place de l'Étoile, honking like hell
round, round the Arch. And gone for good

with wishing . . . Not all the king's men
breaking their balls for years, light years,
could put this story right again.

An American Airman

(Seymour, Connecticut)

Nothing personal. But I hope
once in a blue moon, so help me,
they string all of the niggers up.

Crew Practice
(Lake Bled, in Jugoslavia)
for my son, John

I'd wave the gnats away and try
to tell you, *no one is more dear,*
unable to tell, or think why

and justify our life besides,
hardly in touch. As like that shell's,
fanning water, our shadow glides

down to the dark bottom, beneath
consideration nearly . . . Past
the feudal castle, with each breath

striding much like a galley, or
a leggy water bug, men drop
airs, ages lost in the Great War,

the Austro-Hungarian Empire
and pine island astern—where still
an alpine church upholds its spire

but holds it, also, upside-down
in the water mirror, as though
gravity dragged images down

and drained them off. So many lives.
Caretakers raking the far shore
burn off a winter of wet leaves,

the column of smoke leans. Swallows
blow over all day, worrying
sunset—like quick following harrows

until the sky yields. In widening rings
they orbit, then come back as bats
stroking raggedly on damp wings

(as will the dark, frantic for more,
beat circles over the lamplit
footpath, still darker than before)

equipment in perfect order.

Whenever overtaken, I
duck, nor trust anyone's radar,

not even theirs. Then, when I look
at what comes true, or listen, hard
by the flat tension of a lake

while gooseflesh rises, recalling
how the coxswain's regular bark
marked time, forced rising and falling,

or out of habit dream on Proust,
how little we know or love, those
we know the best and love the most,

then, man to man, this heartless view
tempts me almost to tell a lie,
and wish you better than I do.

The Old Order

sways, blurred horizon breaking up . . .
In the old days our coastguard dory
spluttered and caught—war surplus

on the way out. Father and I
put-putted around the breakwater,
beery, taking our sweet time.

We dropped anchor, fished. Down the coast
a spray of stony islands poked up,
blunt ruins holding their own.

The cottage hugging one of them
for dear life (darkened in the weather)
might have been a love nest, then,

when some landlord could afford it,
or mere retreat for muggy weekends,
the whole family ferried out . . .

Late afternoon, a chill had crept
clear through. Our poles dipped toward the gunnels
as our fingers fell asleep.

Bubbles, fumes, broke from the outboard.
I hauled up the draining bait bucket.
As though flocked before a storm

sailboats, doomed to a monied strut,
took the right of way. Before darkness
they closed in on their yacht club,

the pale canvas or dacron stretched
up almost every mast. Olympian,
we let a handful of them

huffing and puffing into shape
go ahead with their funny weaving
in a maze. Toward the end, they'd

bunch up, uncertain. They would creep
dim and alien, like an orgy
of flowers brushing in a windy field.

Lt. Cmdr. T. E. Sanderson
15 December 1963

None of the brass hatters had seen
the flight plan, nor what orders were,
but judged the thing to be routine.

Part shooting star, the Grumman Tracker
harrowing a suburb . . . It left
headlines. Looked-at hard, the picture

grows atoms, ungathering grains.
He'd come of nothing and made it
after a fashion. What remains

is what to make of him: not torn
out of a dream but living it,
who took-off on Sunday, airborne

in Hingham, Mass. . . . I lie awake
mulling over my mother's note;
embossed, its plumes cap-off the wake:

"just like President Kennedy's,
the American Flag on it
& closed." Not having died at ease

nor in a war, he lay in state,
the case being shut (no news leak
nor angel to uncover it)

and screwed up, sealed the way he went.
All that he was, he had become
by virtue of self government.

The thing is, what to make of it,
of the nation's arms his nation
made of him. Perhaps bit by bit

it all falls together, but then
the thing is Tommy Sanderson
my cousin, fellow citizen,

a uniform of flesh and blood
shoved back into the marshes, down
the Commonwealth, in Hingham mud.

Better to give up, than acquit;
whatever it was he meant
a whole creation weighs on it.

Chicken Country

Here's food for wonder.
No matter what is thrown them
they eat it up.

& their wings, vestigial appendages
like ostrich wings—
they run aground with their heads wrung off.

Come night, the owner throws the switch
& saves the day. Shining,
adrift in space, the coops electrify Connecticut

plastered with feathers, straw & chicken shit,
cinder-blocked lines of unbroken
windows staring in.

The chickens work. It is a factory
where they work their guts out:
shadows in a box, flagging,

who will not let the line die out
but will assemble, reassemble
somewhere along the line.

Still they produce, reproduce
& work as hard as humanly possible.
They work like niggers & are happy—

are equally at home in this
apartment house, this
apartment.

Item: Mrs Chicken finds a red spot
stuck in Mr Chicken's chest.
She pecks at it, pecks

& Mrs Chicken-under-the-skin, clear eyes hard,
steers across the yard. She helps
the little Chickens help their mother peck

until the red red blob pecks back
pecks back
at It

but goes down anyway,
a grand bloody mess
at the end of an August day,

there, right there, in the sea of life
just under the wire.
Life subsides, then. They start from scratch.

Their instincts are sound.
& go on, regardless
whether their great luminary crate

remains an ark, or ocean liner on a holiday
dragging its wake, bearing
row on row of portholes,

a string of naked bulbs,
of china eggs, an egg-necklace,
one current threading day & night.

Walking Around

(Venice)

In memory of Mrs Flo Howard
from Sydney, Australia

The motor throbbing through our soles
droned stilly through the water-taxi.
Freshly painted, wild as maypoles,

gold-capped piles on the Grand Canal
sank in the Lenten air. Also
Salute and the arsenal.

We sat together looking back.
Our launch rocketed toward the Lido.
We fidgeted over smalltalk.

A grade school teacher's holiday . . .
She'd sailed from Down Under, through Suez
to Rome, where her prodigal boy

photographed teen-aged movie queens
jet propelled from America
and sold to movie magazines.

I took her off his hands awhile.
She was dying, but at that time
nobody knew. She tried a smile

that brought me to. The boat docked hard
near the casino. Out of season
we moseyed up a boulevard

gone dark. Flash rains had hit like hail—
our walk lay camouflaged in leaves,
alive with snails. We crushed a snail

at every step. And happened on
the ugly, famous cinema
from which a festival had gone

or had not come. There, on the beach
behind a line of pickets, hung
the candy-striped tents of the rich,

heavy and wet. The fringes stirred
a little, caked with sand. Kind of
stiff. We turned back without a word.

. . . That fall, in Casablanca, I killed
a day on the sundeck, remarking
Arabs thick as flies, and the thrilled

neigh of horses half beat to death,
kicked and dragged up to the gangplank
of a French freighter, stuck for breath,

who let go all over the dock.
That night, walking around down there
I waded through a swarm of cock

roaches. Snug in my bunk, I dreamed
the horses were leaving, calmed, stuffed
in like tinned sardines, as they steamed

off for Marseilles—tons of dog food
no better than a hold of fish—
feeling for sea legs where they stood . . .

My heart pumps like a piston again,
it all comes back to me. And when
I walk as a man among men

or more than a man, or less, even,
I think in the final breakdown
the whole thing will stink to high heaven;

and think of her, between news stands
at the terminal, fat and fifty,
that day I got her off my hands.

I bundled her up on the train
and kissed her off. Bland, round, fuzzy,
the cheek was cooler than peach skin

brushing my lips. Down the packed car
I watched her making her dim way.
At one far compartment door

she hunched down to a nervous cough,
she hesitated in the aisle—
then out of sight, having turned off

and found a place among the crowd.

The Marches

Chemical factories, refineries, puff and overrun.
The railroad bridge's concrete horseshoe arches
plod across the Raritan,

and pink-pale clouds march
as far as the mind can reach, wilting,
central Jersey spread under like spilt milk.

IV

Chiaroscuro

I had almost forgotten you
archaic world,
your subtle turns, your ripe presence,
not false or true
but something to be lived with.

Horns blowing
on the blind curve, we slowed down
stunned by the Umbrian terrain.
Our map unfolded town by town,
mild clouds half vanished into rain
like hill sheep bundled up. As though
settling down, taking hold
the world smoldered,
fog cooling still,
its stunted olive trees born old.

Drained waters twining like a drill
ran down rockface
as though such heights
(nothing but water left to give)
might waste, or fall away
to sights like this—
pale olive dwarfs that live
against the grain,
or the headlong flood below
where calcium and lime
grind one another into mud.

Making headway
our Volks made heavy time
with six of us crouched up for hours,
motion sick. Window and windshield
steamed up, through intermittent
showers . . . Poplars
hazy as pastoral
lounged by an irrigation ditch,
bean-pole towheads
whose shoulders slouched,
letting their wispy cowlicks switch
direction with the wind.

Still, hived
around gnarled axis poles, haystacks
moldered in mounds
like African huts or hills we clung to—
following tracks
foreshortened peasants trudged in rubber boots,
dark umbrellas blown.

Once, a hunter
suddenly edged out of the wood
to strike a match.
With a shotgun,
breech broken on the arm, he stood
smoking there,
sconced in a tableau
where nothing stands up from the earth
but slumps a little, doing so.

Interminable forest,
a wooden mood the sun dispels . . .
My wife's cheekbones
as by a wand were touched with fire
once, our friends' skulls
crowned with blond hair, their children blond.

There had already been a birth,
and we drove on
up to Assisi. Coming on
Giotto's *Flight Into Egypt*: gloss
smoked off the holy refugees,
they long for exile, and they'd cross
that dislocated waste of faults
between hill towns,
the dense sky blue
as only heaven-painted vaults
are blue. What were they fleeing to?
One angel steadfast forward, one
still gazing back, Herod behind,
the Cross ahead. Or even
lion-headed Egypt, gone
with sand blown, crawling in her lap,
stone blind.

Dust in the Vatican Museum.

White milestones come on, bleak,
and silvery olive trees—
dear crones in a dream
of agony, too old to speak.

What belvederes we'd improvised!
Whole lands rambled in tapestries
where nothing will be recognized,
not plots grown wild
nor orchard trees turned gold,
but cypress, the dark leaf, the peaked
cumulus of mold,
a patch of grief . . .

High up, from its square-eyed monk's cowl
the medieval bell tower tolls
over the woods, where wolves still prowl,
a swollen Angelus that rolls
around the hills . . .
They rise in cloud.
Whatever they expect of us
is more than us,
and we are cowed as we are moved
superfluous
toward Rome, the blacktop stretch laid bare.
Alert goats hover in the dusk.

Carabinieri from nowhere
swoop down on us,
both goggle-masked
and helmeted, like New World nuns
traveling in pairs.
For a short while
the tires whine and sing.
Each guns his motorcycle,
single file, and then
abreast in olive uniforms,
messengers, who with a last fling
fan out in front,
their wheeling forms
fading before us, wing and wing.

I Frammenti

(Brela, Dalmacija)
In memory of Stipin Juričić,
his family & their hospitality

1.
Snapshot

Stipin at 74
still poses
paterfamilias stiff
in lavender light

having his picture snapped.
Badly mended
cracked spectacles
gravitate down his nose.

Up the smudged backsliding folds of road
serpentina, a woman tugs
a fat bladdered goat
who hobbles through the dust

an avalanche of pebbles
dragged out at the heels . . .
Stipin's wife.
Unprobed, cancer

mushrooms in her voluminous black blouse, under
the mound of dry goods,
no disaster
but the fact of life.

Beyond all that,
buoyant
on homemade wine and pride
the old man will wave good-bye

babbling broken Italian:
Quan ritorn tu
saro nel
Paradiso.

2.
Memento Mori

Coastal hills
volleyed cuckoo echoes.
They backed us up. They
cut us off from the interior.

The covering of pine trees
the fragrancy
died
down along the beach.

Hollow
hoarse
a jackass hee-hawed
airing the dry heaves.

Raked-over shingle
rattled into the Adriatic
quietly clapping its bones.
No matter

what stones we scaled
how flat
how many times
they dropped out of sight.

Even the washed up sea urchin,
a raspberry-speckled egg
shocked with spines
like a contact mine

crumbled,
powdering our palms . . .
Islands
flourished offshore

virtual Hesperides,
and the miniature
motor driven ferry
running out like a series of duds

touched back and forth, and forth,
suddenly snuffed,
so undependable
we could depend on it.

3.
"UN COUP DE DÉS"

Night, night. Stipin
fiddles with short wave radio
tuned in
to news from over the water.

Out for a breath of air
among the pines' antennae
I clear my head.
Both up and down

the scattered, vaguely whited houses
lodge at a tilt
like chunks off the moon
coming to this,

no village
but a settlement,
where the lime-riddled stone roofs
hold up

as if by pure luck
or less,
a throw of highlights
on the heavily wooded rise.

Blueberries

"The feast is all around us."
—G.C.

Up in a clearing of the wood, beyond
the wavering incline behind our house
—wild among scrub and poison ivy—
we find the high bush variety.

Hung in the hot, sticky air
under the leaves,
in two's, and three's, and one's,
each delicate worldly sphere appears
refrigerated, fresh—a full one
dusted with blueish, flat-finish mist.
It picks up fingerprints.
(The gentle brutes rub through, as though
accidentally polishing the genie's lamp.
Patches of deeper blue break out, ragged,
and galaxies glimmer in the distance . . .)

Juggled, bruised,
piled in the bucket, they burst
with diminutive spiky tufts; they leave
an impression of darkness shiny with use—
a heap of old ball bearings wearing through the grease.

And we have clung, like these.
                                        Consider.
Off in an otherworld—the end of *this* world
clarified by perspective—
obscure, rotating sentinels
hold smoothly to the dazzling capitals, the columns;
they have turned their shoulders to the wheel
wearing shoulders down. Too soon,
even planets wobble under astronomical laws . . .
After 29 years of rage
my belly drops into rampant midde age.

Our vulnerability remains, the saving grace.
Lost in an unspectacular cranny,
battered, manhandled,
we are neither false nor true.
O blueberries, whose blood is juice! All together—
who entertain, perhaps, an aftertaste
of the banal, heartfelt, metaphysical abyss
reaching up and cutting through.

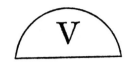

"All flesh *is* grass."—ISAIAH

Sunrise

Like an old comedian, one expects to go on forever,
rolled over and over until the dream
he is in Paradise. It is a bedroom
furnished Empire-style:
on the dresser, a mirror fit for Versailles
overlooks the whole spectrum of vanities;
a network of goldleaf scrollwork
dredges the white paint,
assuming a rose hue. The sun
no longer flushed or faint
comes hard and clear: here

bundled home after a long night
like Messalina, the nymphomaniac
(Claudius, the husband, still asleep,
and Juvenal, the conscience, unheard-of)
urged up out of the cold brine, sweaty,
having broken faith, having kept faith
neither in love nor hate, which do not abide,
but arising, refreshed,
so that it slips across the room
and beams in the way of an ordinary life,
everyone's wife.

Provinces

Darker than any monument,

before the charm of reasons,
one blood runs through the *Iliad*:

                              the unstrung heroes
had fathers and mothers who loved them, ignorant,
in another place, another time
adoring the tireless light of a burnt-out star

off in a distant corner of the world.

The Grandson

There goes the grandson, run off to the beach!
It's *me!* Canary trolleys in a daze
round a corner, parade through blocks of days,
walking on eggs. Spirited out of reach . . .

At each wand's live tip, a stunning wheel leads
blue electrical sparks. They jump the wire—
meteorites, confetti of dying fire.
Clang. Clang. Turned off, then, in flourishing weeds.

I whistled toward the sea . . . *A manikin*
whose pores pinked and closed, a glowing disease.
Evenings, I fell in with the cool sea-breeze
while secret fevers riffled through my skin . . .

Aeons ago! Now, everything depends.
Tugged inside-out like a sweater, all seams,
one is less definite. A cinder. Age seems
a matter of finding yourself at loose ends.

I make for anarchy, the final coup.
But who goes there? What cast-off human fate
runs away to sea? I see. I see! Wait,
wait for me, dear old days! I'm coming too.

Pier

(Lake Sunapee, Mt. Sunapee, New Hampshire)

A race, perhaps. You might have called it that
when the cavalier Lightnings tilted: your camera
with a spool at either end
reeled, unreeled,
a day's adventure starting out . . .

and the wind thuds, hauling through broad lily pads,
scouring the water-top. Off, off the bank
an oilskin poncho dripping wet
puffs up, *brilliant,*

a sudden breath. The dead
power launches tug their mooring lines.
Sunapee, mirrored mountain, moving or moved
shivers and swoons

         out there.

                Reflexive sails
heel at the red buoy, flagging, and even out
or tack closer, trimmed to a fresh send-off
(whose humdrum tread is measured in review)
their crisp bell-bottoms ballooning, flapped out
as they skim over in a long, lean glide,
the ceremony of the following wind
caught in mid-stride . . .

the camera humming to itself. The small
dark mind adjusts, taking all of it in,
for here you are, for *that* is how it feels
and it's good to be alive, a white-capped green
kaleidoscope of far flung, farfetched sails
dipping and rocking.

                    And never, not even
in your wildest dreams, will you arrive.

Facing Up

A croak out of the marsh in the dark hollow,
drowned chord roaming.
It broke into our sleep.

                    Then
this March morning, plopped in the dooryard—
that old familiar amphibian

marooned on the crabgrass (a more rugged green)
unmoving, and bigger than life
being blurted out.

                Unbeautiful
who turned up, perhaps, for air.

. . . It is the Frog Prince
under a spell of wishing, just under
a cold archaic smile,

having come so far, in mottled skin
green and darker green
like dappled leaf, sick, bewitched,

through shades, through clammy depth
coming to be kissed.

Graven Images

Aaron Scully
Dec. 12, 1965
June 2, 1966

1.

He went on,
            Aaron to Zion—
the Errand into the Wilderness.

                              Again
a New World blooms in the Book of the Dead.

Here, even Puritans turn to images,
vernacular, flat, abstracted
engravings in slate.
                    So unnatural
they're something else again.

Heads fly, or seem to.
                    But whose?
Souls giddy in effigy, a humbled bee-like bliss?
Or Death's head ragged at the lip?

                              A man can hardly tell
the wings of this or that triumph.

Neither might the stonecutter
looking into his heart, discover.

                              Tentative
between Time and Eternity, let us say,
in carved doorway, gateway, arch or portal,
these are the frozen souls
                    on the ruined way.

Eyes brighten, webs of lichen—already
intimate as the Crab Nebula;
wonderful fish mouths, O's, sucking for air
evolving everywhere . . .

Kilroy faces wedged in storybook wings.

2.

Aaron, smothered in clear plastic,
you were not in the best of hands.
Not then, not ever.

              Listen. We have elected
President Death. He delivers
ghost writing on invisible glass.

                  . . . After, after ages
under that careless elemental government,
the hand of your father, of *mine*

year after year more saturnine . . .
this moment, this

marble will sugar over, as it must,
the plot choke with clover and dust.

3.

Take care, dear. Take care.

              Wherever,
however mind or heart may take their stands—
at court of law or others,

           in love or fever,
our life is in these almost-human hands.

NOTES & EXPLANATIONS

"Aimai-je un rêve?"

The title ("Loved I a dream?") is from Mallarmé's *"L'Après-midi d'un faune."*

An American Airman (Northern France)

The "Arch" or *Arc de Triomphe* stands at the hub of the "Place de l'Étoile," the place of the star, of destiny.

An American Airman (Seymour, Connecticut)

The precedent for this poem, and in part its origin, is a documentary lyric by Archilochus (seventh-century B.C. poet and mercenary soldier), specifically the fragment that Richmond Lattimore translates:

We, a thousand, are the murderers of the seven men who fell dead. We overtook them with our running feet. . . .

Crew Practice

The eleventh-century "feudal castle" is now a museum. The "alpine church"—situated on the tiny island that was once supposed to be the home of Živa, a Slav goddess of love and life—has been secularized.

Chicken Country

"Connecticut," a word of Indian origin, is usually taken to mean "on the long tidal river."

Walking Around

"Salute" (sah-loo-tay), which means Salvation, is a church on the Grand Canal.

Chiaroscuro

Touring Umbria and Tuscany.
"Carabinieri": Italian gendarmes; carabineers.

I Frammenti

The fragments, pieces, what-have-you.

"Quan . . . Paradiso": "When you return I'll be in Paradise."

"UN COUP DE DÉS" ("A THROW OF THE DICE") is the title of a poem by Mallarmé.

Blueberries

In the penultimate line: "banal" should be pronounced bay-nəl.

Graven Images

Although the title derives ultimately from *Exodus,* it was brought to mind and qualified by Allan I. Ludwig's *Graven Images* (Wesleyan, 1966), a study of early New England funerary sculpture.

"Neither" is used in the sense of "nor."

James Scully was born in New Haven in 1937. He was educated at the University of Connecticut where presently he teaches in its Department of English. Mr. Scully was the recipient of an Ingram Merrill Foundation Fellowship in 1962 to write poetry. His poems have appeared in *The New Yorker, Poetry, The Floating Opera,* and other magazines. He is the editor of *Modern Poetics* (1965). *The Marches* is Mr. Scully's first book of poems.